THE SOUL OF

SAINT NICHOLAS

by

Douglas James Joyce

Cover illustration by Stela Casian

For Mr. and Mrs. Claus

IT WAS THE NIGHT before Christmas, and all through the land, people were reading the news:

Anchorage Confirms Santa's Departure

ANCHORAGE, AK — Radar screens at Air Traffic Control here, lit up like Christmas trees last night as an unidentified flying object entered American skies at 11:53 PST.

A chase squadron of three F-104 Starfighters was immediately dispatched.

The jets screamed toward their target at twice the speed of sound. Soon, the pilots could make out a red glow cutting through the wintry Yukon sky. They drew nearer and surrounded the target in 'escort formation'.

The enemy craft was later described by one of the pilots as "an old man at the controls of a sleigh and nine reindeer, movin' south like greased lightning." The sleigh appeared to be heavily laden with cargo.

A cheery "Merry Christmas, gentlemen!" was received by the three astonished pilots, who returned a 'thumbs up' to the jolly old man in the red suit. As the fighters broke off and regrouped, Anchorage ATC confirmed the sighting of St. Nicholas, wished him a good flight, and handed him off to Juneau.[1]

So Santa Claus was coming to town, but how did he get here? The story begins a long time ago, in a little town far, far away — in a place called Patara, a once-bustling port on the eastern shores of the Mediterranean Sea.

People said Patara had been founded by Patarus, son of Lycia and Apollo. The Sun-god — revealer of past, present, and future, god of sun and light, music and poetry, truth and prophecy — had established a seasonal oracle at Patara, second only to Delphi in importance. It was during the winter months alone that a priestess of the temple at Patara would speak for Apollo, when seekers from far and wide could request his divination.

But Apollo's ancient temple was already in ruins when Epiphanes the Illustrious and Johane, a devout and wealthy couple, begat a son "in the first flower of their age."[2] As Michael the Archimandrite, the earliest known biographer of Saint Nicholas, records, "Since their wishes were in accord with God's, at the first coupling with each other there was conceived a fruit of righteousness."[3] Or it may have been a "manifestation of God" named Theophanes and his wife Nonna who were finally blessed with child after many years of barrenness, when the prayers of Nonna were at last answered like those of Hannah in the Bible's Old Testament, imploring God to give his handmaid a baby boy so she could in turn give him unto the Lord all the days of his life.[4]

Both are wonderful stories, and at least one of them must be true, for a boychild was born in Patara on the ides of March in the year of our Lord 270. He was christened Nicholas, which is Greek for "people's victory," after his uncle Nicholas, the abbot of a local monastery.[5]

Like all firstborn boys bound for the priesthood, Nicholas immediately demonstrated great piety. Some say that upon his baptism, the infant Nicholas stood up in the basin, raised his little arms to heaven and cried out to the Lord above,[6] which must have been something to see indeed. Others say the babe would take his mother's teat only on Wednesdays and Fridays, and then only once each day, allowing himself to suckle according to priestly rule rather than the desires of his tummy.[7] This latter claim may, of course, be apocryphal.

Yet the boy's piety and steadfast love of the catholic church undoubtedly continued to grow, and "on her teachings he enlightened his mind daily, divinely elevating it to the pure and truest devotion."[8]

How enthralled he must have been to learn about the Acts of the Apostles, how Saint Paul himself, serving the Lord with all humility of mind, had sailed from Rhodes after his ordeal in Greece, saying, *I have shewed you all things, how that so labouring ye ought to support the weak, and to remember the words of the Lord Jesus, how he said, "It is more blessed to give than to receive."* The Apostle had then sailed right into Patara, where he boarded a ship bound for Phenicia, and made his way back to Jerusalem and the Holy Land, nearly two hundred years before. So Nicholas assiduously avoided the company of crude boys and kept his virginity intact. Then tragedy struck. A contagion raced through all of Lycia, wresting away young and old, rich and poor, pious and pagan alike. The lad was spared, but both of his parents succumbed to the plague, leaving Nicholas an orphan to be raised by his uncle in the monastery, and having only God as his father.[9]

Since his parents had been quite wealthy, they left Nicholas with a substantial sum of money, which his uncle kept in safekeeping until such time as the boy was ready to enter the priesthood and would no longer need such worldly riches. And when the time came to don his priestly vestments, Nicholas determined that he must not lay up his treasures on earth but must lay up his treasure in heaven, for, as it is written by Saint Matthew, *where your treasure is, there will your heart be also.* Yet how was he to do so? The young man "firmly begged the good God that he surrender his life and all his possessions, if that seemed good to Him,"[10] and he took to heart the injunction of Jesus, in his Sermon on the Mount, *that ye do not your alms before men, to be seen of them: otherwise ye have no reward of your Father which is in heaven.* So Nicholas resolved to serve up his inheritance as alms to the poor, and he further resolved to do so in secret. His Father alone would witness these acts of almsgiving.

Now, there was a poor man living nearby who had three daughters but no dowry. The man had been well-born and was once wealthy yet had recently fallen upon hard times. His daughters were all comely, but without dowry no man would stoop to marriage with them. The family had become destitute, and the man had at last considered the egregious act of committing his daughters into a brothel, just so the family could eat. As the family lived in the neighborhood, Nicholas soon learned of their plight and the father's decision to sell his own children into sin and servitude. "But the Lord who loves humankind, who never wishes his own creation to become hostage to sin, sent him a holy angel — I mean the godlike Nicholas — both to rescue him, along with his whole household, from poverty and destruction, and to restore readily his previous prosperity."[11] Thus the devout young Nicholas devised a plan whereby he could assist the family without their knowledge; he would provide for them in such a way "that thine alms should be in secret."

And so late that night, under cover of darkness, when all through the house not a creature was stirring, Nicholas walked along the dark alleyways of Patara. He found an open window and, while all were sound asleep, he tossed a bag of gold coins into the poor family's home, then quickly, quietly stole away into the night. Some say the bag fell into a stocking that had been hung to dry, while others claim the bag landed in a shoe. All the same, when the family discovered their gift the next morning, they were overcome with joy. The father immediately put up a dowry for his eldest daughter, and he secured her hand in marriage to a good man, one who would support her and care for her for the rest of her life.

Nicholas heard the good news and determined to assist the second daughter as well. Again he waited until all were asleep to toss a bag of gold into the family's home before speeding away, undiscovered and unknown, under cover of darkness. Again the family rejoiced the next morning, and again their father set up a dowry, this time for his second daughter, and secured for her a good man in marriage.

Now this father hoped and prayed that similar salvation would be granted his third daughter, and he resolved to discover the identity of the family's patron, their holy angel. That night, he made sure the window was open and sat up to await the longed-for night visitor. Unfortunately, he soon fell fast asleep, but when he heard the tinkling jingle of gold coins tossed once more into their home, he was startled awake. He ran out into the darkness to apprehend his benefactor and finally caught up with Nicholas in the alley, hastily making his way back home. "When he recognized who he was, he threw himself face-first at his feet with cries, and gave thanks to him over and over with many words and called him his and his three daughters' savior, after God, and said, 'If our common Master, Christ, hadn't stirred your goodness, we would have long ago destroyed our own lives by a shameful and destructive livelihood.'"[12] But Nicholas would have none of it, and he required the man "not to tell nor discover this thing as long as he lived."[13] Nevertheless, like that of the leper whom Jesus cleansed on his way back from the Mount of Beatitudes, the story of the young man's secret charity could not be silenced. The seed of giving in secret had been planted in good soil. It there took root, and was now sprung up:

This Flower whose fragrance tender
With sweetness fills the air
Dispels with glorious splendor
The darkness everywhere.[14]

HAVING DIVESTED HIMSELF OF worldly treasure, Nicholas could now complete his training for the priesthood, which he did by means of a pilgrimage to the Holy Land, following in the very footsteps of Jesus. While touring the little town of Bethlehem, he even slept in a grotto that may have resembled the stable where Saint Luke says the Blessed Virgin Mary *brought forth her firstborn son, and wrapped him in swaddling clothes, and laid him in a manger; because there was no room for them in the inn.* We can just imagine the devout young Nicholas standing in the grotto that night, reenacting in his own mind the Nativity scene: the little lord Jesus asleep on the hay, with Joseph and Mary, so meek and so mild; the Magi bearing gifts of gold and frankincense and myrrh while shepherds quake at the sight; the ox and lamb and even the donkey, shaggy and brown, that carried his mother up hill and down.

In Jerusalem, Nicholas evoked the Way of Sorrows by first visiting the upper room where Jesus and the Twelve took their Last Supper. Where Jesus proclaimed, "He that is greatest among you shall be your servant," then poured a basin of water and washed the feet of each of his disciples to underscore the point, while Judas Iscariot cringed at this unseemly display and finally settled his mind upon betrayal. Nicholas then went trudging up Golgotha, that is, Mount Calvary, where Jesus of Nazareth suffered and died on the cross — *Behold the*

Savior of mankind Nailed to the shameful tree![15] — and down again to the Holy Sepulchre,[16] where Saint Mark says Joseph of Arimathaea laid the crucified body of Jesus *in a sepulchre which was hewn out of a rock, and rolled a stone unto the door of the sepulchre.* Having thus completed his indoctrination, Nicholas returned to Patara, where he was immediately "advanced to a pastoral dignity" and placed "on a high-priestly lamp-stand as a brilliantly shining lamp for the salvation of many."[17] He was, after all, Nicholas — the people's victory.

Shortly after donning his vestments, Father Nicholas was called to serve the nearby Metropolis of Myra, also on the Mediterranean coast. As fortune would have it, the leader of that church soon "left behind his earthly pursuits and traveled to God,"[18] leaving his fellow bishops at a loss as to how to fill this vacancy in the church at Myra. So they fasted and they prayed, and one of them, a great bishop high in authority, "heard that night a voice which said to him that, at the hour of matins, he should take heed to the doors of the church, and him that should come first to the church, and have the name of Nicholas they should *sacre* him bishop."[19] And so that night they took heed and kept their vigil at the door of the church, and just after midnight who should come rushing into the house of prayer but our young priest. They inquired of his name, and when he replied, "I am Nicholas," the bishops understood that he had been sent by God, and they forthwith commenced the Rite of Election and placed upon his shoulders the bishop's gown: a scarlet robe trimmed in snow white fur.

When the people of Myra heard the news that their beloved Nicholas had been elected bishop of their church, they rejoiced and required "the people's victory" to mount the bishop's throne. Thus Nicholas "became the best shepherd of Christ's rational creatures, he who was approved by Him and designated by name[.]"[20] And he instructed his flock in perfect orthodoxy, "apostolically teaching them to worship God the Father and his only-born Word and Son, our Lord and God Jesus Christ, and the Spirit."[21] He professed to them the truth of the Holy Trinity — its unity, equality, and harmony — that is, "one God known in three persons, co-eternal and undivided, whose three specific characters are not, because of the oneness of their nature, coalesced into one person, as foolish Sabellius would have it, nor is their divine and uncreated perfect divinity divided into three alien and unrelated essences because of their triple personhood, as accursed Arius would have it."[22] Nicholas taught the congregation well.

Then tragedy again struck the land, this time in the form of great famine, leaving rich and poor alike with no grain to eat or sow. Therefore, when Nicholas saw three ships come sailing into the harbor laden with wheat, he hastened down to the docks to plead with their captains that they might sell some of the grain in order to alleviate the people's hunger. The mariners replied, "Father, we dare not, for it is meted and measured, and we must give reckoning thereof in the garners of the Emperor in Alexandria. And the holy man said to them: 'Do this that I have said to you, and I promise, in the truth of God, that it shall not be lessened or diminished when ye shall come to the garners.'"[23] So the captains ordered that some of the shipment be offloaded, yet when they later docked at Alexandria, they found that their holds contained as much wheat as before landing at Myra. They recounted this wonder to the ministers of the Emperor, and the story of the Bishop of Myra began to be recited all around the Mediterranean Sea, and every sailor who told the tale made sure to depict the saint in his distinctive fur-trimmed robe of red. And so it was that the soul of Saint Nicholas first began to fly: on the winds that drove the barks that sailed the Mediterranean, the center of the Christian world.

Meanwhile, back in Myra, the holy bishop worked long and hard in overseeing the equitable distribution of the wheat that he had procured, ensuring that every man, woman, and child had enough to eat. There was, in fact, sufficient grain such that in the springtime, the people "kept some of it for sowing and scattered it in their fields, and thus enjoyed God's kindnesses through the entreaties of his holy servant Nicholas."[24] And they rejoiced in recalling Saint Paul's words to the people of Corinth: *And now abideth faith, hope, charity, these three; but the greatest of these is charity.* Charity is truly the gift that keeps on giving.

THEN IN THE YEAR of the Lord 303, the Roman Emperor Diocletian became enraged by the growing number of Christians who refused to worship in the temples of Jupiter, Mars, and Apollo. Worse, these Christians refused to recognize the emperor himself as their god. So he undertook a program of persecuting the Christians, ordering his battalions to kill or imprison all those who would not mouth obeisance to their emperor god in Rome. Churches were destroyed. Services were banned. Scriptures were burned.[25] And Nicholas was among those swept up in the madness. The Roman soldiers were quick to cast him into prison for refusing to renounce the Holy Trinity of Father, Son, and Spirit.

While the Bishop of Myra languished in his cell, the soul of Saint Nicholas continued to fly throughout the Roman world, borne aloft by the men who sailed the sea and told his story wherever they landed. When they returned to Myra, they saw firsthand the fruits of the bishop's charity. They saw prosperity in place of poverty. They saw plenty where there had once been famine. Then they sailed to Patara, where they heard the story of how young Nicholas had saved a family from destitution, sin, and servitude through his charitable acts of giving alms in secret. They even heard the legend of his extraordinary baptism. And so they magnified the hero of their wondrous story and, though humble Nicholas would certainly have disapproved, these sailors took him as their patron saint, calling upon him to protect them from those barking sea-hounds of Scylla as they plied the waters of Sicily, and beseeching him to help steer a safe course around the terrible sucking waves of Charybdis. And whenever they found safe harbor after an arduous sea crossing, these grateful sailors would praise their Saint Nicholas and relate his story to whomever would listen.

Fortunately, the reign of Diocletian the Persecutor would end in only a couple of years, as he abdicated in 305 *anno domini*. His successor would be that great and powerful visionary, the Emperor Constantine, who, like all visionaries, was blessed with an open mind. Though Constantine was not entirely persuaded by its theology, he could see quite clearly that fighting the rise of Christianity would be a losing battle, one that he was unwilling to fight. Besides, his mother Helena was a Christian convert who had recently toured the Holy Land, where she claimed to have found the True Cross of Christ. So Constantine ordered the prison gates to be opened, and he released all those persecuted by Diocletian, including the Bishop of Myra. Constantine may not have declared himself head of this new and vibrant religion, but he did intend to guide and manage it. And, while the emperor may have been open-minded, he nevertheless could not abide the fractious squabbling that the bishops reverted to upon their release.

So in the year 325 AD, the Roman Emperor Constantine called leaders from all of Christendom to meet in Nicaea, in what is now northern Turkey, not far from his new capital, Constantinople. The aging Bishop of Myra is said to have made the long journey, along with some 300 other bishops and church leaders, though his name appears only in later recordings of what has come to be known as the First Council of Nicaea. As was their wont, the bishops immediately fell to wrangling over doctrine, and that accursed Arius of Alexandria was among the loudest, ranting his outrageous position that the Holy Trinity was not one, but rather "three alien and unrelated essences because of their triple personhood."[26] Well, the Bishop of Myra had had just about all he could take of such heresy, so he walked right up to Arius and delivered him a smack in the face. The entire assembly was aghast at his effrontery, so they defrocked Nicholas on the spot, thus relegating him to the sidelines for the remainder of the council. It does seem, however, that Constantine and nearly all the other bishops may have secretly applauded the Bishop of Myra for finally ending the diatribe of Arius because when it came to a vote, all but two of the bishops sided with Nicholas. And so it is that to this day we recite the Nicene Creed in the manner that Saint Nicholas would have it:

> **I believe in one God, the Father Almighty, Maker of heaven and earth and of all things visible and invisible.**
>
> **And in one Lord Jesus Christ, the only-begotten Son of God, begotten of His Father before all worlds, God of God, Light of Light, Very God of Very God, Begotten, not made, Being of one**

substance with the Father, By whom all things were made[....][27]

When the First Council finally adjourned, the fur-trimmed robe of red was once more placed upon the shoulders of the Bishop of Myra, while Arius and the two bishops who sided with his heretical position were banished to Illyria, there to live among the Goths and pirates of the Balkans. Our Nicholas, the people's victory, had carried the day.

He returned to Myra, where he dedicated his entire being to charitable almsgiving. It seemed that wherever a need arose, Nicholas was always there to fill it. Moreover, as one of his monks related to Michael the Archimandrite, "Nicholas was as follows: venerable and angelic in appearance, and exuding sweet smells full of sanctification, so that just at the sight of him he improved those who were with him and pushed and changed them to a better state which bordered on salvation."[28] Nevertheless, the years eventually caught up with Nicholas, as they do to us all, and there came a time when he "prayed our Lord that he would send him his angels; and inclining his head he saw the angels come to him, whereby he knew well that he should depart[.]"[29] And so, praying, "'Lord, into thine hands I commend my spirit,' Nicholas rendered up his soul and died, the year of our Lord three hundred and forty-three, with great melody sung of the celestial company."[30] Nicholas of Myra passed away on the Sixth of December, the date on which many now observe his feast day.[31] The grieving people of Myra lay their beloved bishop to rest within his own church, in a sepulcher which was hewn out of marble, yet he was not to lie there long. The soul of Saint Nicholas had long since been flying across the sea. His bones would soon be setting sail as well.

MARAUDING TURKS EVENTUALLY DESTROYED Myra in the name of Allah, but the bishop remained safe in his sepulcher until the times of the new millennium, when there arose a need for his presence in Christian Europe. Across the

Adriatic Sea there lay a bustling port city called Bari, on the very heel of Italy's boot. The good people of Bari, which means "servant of the Creator" in the original Arabic, were in a bit of a bind. They were building a mighty fortress of a church, the Pontifical Basilica di San Nicola, in honor of their patron saint, but they possessed no sacred relics. What's a basilica without relics? It's a joke! Then city leaders got wind of some Venetians planning to mount an attack on Myra and claim the remains of Nicholas for their own. Venice had enough already! The remains of Saint Mark the Evangelist had been transferred to Venice two hundred years prior, so they already had an apostle, for Christ's sake. Besides, the Venetians were merchants and moneylenders; what did they need with the patron saint of sailors? So in the year 1087 AD, the people of Bari assembled a team of 47 knights who hastily sailed across the Adriatic and down the coast of Turkey to transfer the remains of Nicholas to Bari.[32]

When the knights arrived in Myra, they were surprised to find the ancient city undefended. They interrogated four loitering monks, who readily led the knights to the sepulcher where Nicholas lay. Still feeling apprehensive about Venetians on their tail, as well as the ever-present threat of avenging Turks, the knights hurriedly pried the marble lid off the tomb and scooped up the skeletal remains they found within. Then, nervously looking over their shoulders as they ran with their booty of bones, the tomb raiders beat a hasty retreat to the boats waiting at anchor in the harbor. Having now won their prize, and under his divine protection, they sailed swiftly back to Bari, where the people rejoiced at the interment of their patron saint in the glorious crypt built specially to house him for all of eternity. With its marvelous Basilica di San Nicola and sacred relics, the city of Bari would now become an important pilgrimage destination, attracting Roman Catholics and Orthodox Christians from around the Mediterranean, across Eastern Europe and even parts of Asia, for nearly a thousand years. And that is how Nicholas of Myra came to be known as San Nicola di Bari.

UPON LANDING IN ITALY, San Nicola soon began stealthily walking the streets again, just as Nicholas had done in Patara, nearly a thousand years before. As the soul of Saint Nicholas traveled north on the tongues of the monks and friars that fanned out across all of Europe carrying the good news, it became customary for children to receive gifts on Saint Nicholas Day. And in his wake there always followed glorious music: from the contrapuntal Christmas *motets* of the Renaissance composer known as Palestrina, to hymns calling the faithful with "Adeste Fideles." The songs were sung in Latin, the olden language of the church, which the people could no longer understand, let alone read, yet when set to music, joyous strains of *gloria in excelsis Deo* are readily understood by all. *Glory to God in the highest!*

After crossing the High Alps, the soul of Saint Nicholas began to walk beside fruitful vineyards on the roadways of France while leading a little donkey laden with baskets of gifts, cookies, and sweets for all the good little boys and girls on Saint Nicholas Day. In much of France, Nicholas has come to be known as *Père Noël,* or Father Christmas, and his donkey is often followed by the frightening specter of *Père Fouettard,* or Father Whipper, a dark and dirty fellow with a filthy gray beard who brandishes a whip and disciplines all the boys and girls that have misbehaved during the year.[33]

In French convents, young girls would often hear priests intone the story of Christ's birth in readings from the Latin Vulgate Bible at Mass:

ET PASTORES ERANT IN REGIONE EADEM VIGILANTES, ET CUSTODIENTES VIGILIAS NOCTIS SUPER GREGEM SUUM. ET ECCE ANGELUS DOMINI STETIT JUXTA ILLOS, ET CLARITAS DEI CIRCUMFULSIT ILLOS, ET TIMUERUNT TIMORE MAGNO. ET DIXIT

ILLIS ANGELUS : NOLITE TIMERE : ECCE
ENIM EVANGELIZO VOBIS GAUDIUM
MAGNUM, QUOD ERIT OMNI POPULO : QUIA
NATUS EST VOBIS HODIE SALVATOR, QUI
EST CHRISTUS DOMINUS, IN CIVITATE
DAVID.

But who can understand that? It might as well be Greek! Then the girls would listen with rapt attention to friars telling the story of how Saint Nicholas had once saved three young women from lives of poverty and prostitution through his charitable acts of secret almsgiving. Now that was a story they could relate to! Many of these girls had undoubtedly been rescued from similar straits themselves. So on Saint Nicholas Eve the girls would hang stockings on the fireplace mantel as if to dry, then pray that Nicholas would secretly leave gifts for them also.[34] And as the stockings were hung by the fireplace with care, the girls may have reflected upon the birth of Jesus and the promise of redemption by singing songs like the beautiful and wondrous "Cantique de Noël" ("O Holy Night"):

O holy night! The stars are brightly shining,

It is the night of our dear Saviour's birth.

Long lay the world in sin and error pining,

Till He appear'd and the soul felt its worth.

A thrill of hope, the weary world rejoices,

For yonder breaks a new and glorious morn.

AS THE SOUL OF Saint Nicholas moved across Europe into Belgium and Holland, he became known as *Sinterklaas,* a linguistic corruption of *Saint Nicholas* in which "saint" became "sinter" and "Nicholas" took the diminutive form "Klaas" (similar to the German diminutive "Klaus" for "Nikolaus"). While his name may have become diminutive, his donkey morphed into a horse named Amerigo that carries the bishop from his home in Spain — a consequence of prior Spanish rule over the region — where Sinterklaas spends the year making a list of who's been naughty and nice before returning on his feast day. In anticipation of his arrival, children sing Sinterklaas songs while they await the bishop, who comes wearing a red cape and mitre. Sinterklaas is accompanied by numerous imps known as "Zwarte Pieten" or *Black Petes* — sooty little chimney sweeps that slip down the chimney and deliver gifts to children who have left a boot in front of the fireplace before going to bed. The children often slip a carrot into their boot for Amerigo, the bishop's horse, and in return Black Pete leaves them tasty treats or a small toy — if they were nice. If the children were naughty, Black Pete stuffs them into a sack and carries them off to Spain.[35] Black Pete takes the jolly yuletide admonition to *be good for goodness' sake* to an entirely different level.

AND STILL THE SOUL of Saint Nicholas traveled on, following the Rhine into the heart of Germany, where at the turn of the 14th century, during the times of the Holy Roman Empire, the

German theologian, philosopher, and mystic known as Meister Eckhart taught his flock that

Saint Augustine says: "The soul becomes like that which it loves. If it loves earthly things, then it becomes earthly." We might ask: if it loves God, does it then become God? If I said that, it would sound incredible to those whose understanding is too limited to grasp this. But Augustine says: "I do not say it, but I refer you to Scripture, where we read: 'I have said that you are gods.'"[36]

The Psalmist would conclude his song by declaring that "all of you are children of the Most High" (Psalms 82:6). With this, Meister Eckhart could connect this extraordinary scripture to the Christmas story, proclaiming that "the Father gives birth to his sole-begotten Son in a perpetual present and the soul is herself born again into God. Every time this birth takes place, the sole-begotten Son is born. Therefore, there are far more sons born to virgins than are born to married women, for the former give birth above time in eternity."[37]

About two centuries later, an Augustinian monk and professor of theology named Martin Luther brought the esoteric teachings of Meister Eckhart down to earth for his congregants in Wittenberg. Over the course of his many Christmas sermons, Luther separately examined each of the characters in the Nativity Story, using his own German translation of the original Greek gospels because, he says, "We must both read and meditate upon the Nativity."[38] In his lesson on the Annunciation, Luther paraphrases the angel Gabriel, saying,

> *"Mary, you have asked too high a question for me, but the Holy Spirit will come upon you and the power of the Most High will overshadow you and you will not know yourself how it happens." Had she not believed, she could not have conceived. She held fast to the word of the angel because she had become a new creature. Even so must we be transformed and renewed in heart from day to day.*[39]

On the Nativity itself, a scene that Saint Nicholas had envisioned over a thousand years prior, Luther focused on the lack of assistance offered to Mary as she went into labor and delivered the baby Jesus, saying,

> *There are many of you in this congregation who think to yourselves: "If only I had been there! How quick I would have been to help the Baby! I would have washed his linen. How happy I would have been to go with the shepherds to see the Lord lying in the manger!" Yes, you would! You say that because you know how great Christ is, but if you had been there at that time you would have done no better than the people of Bethlehem. Childish and silly thoughts are these! Why don't you do it now? You have Christ in your neighbor. You ought to serve him, for what you do to your neighbor in need you do to the Lord Christ himself.[40]*

In his lesson on Shepherds *abiding in the field, keeping watch over their flock by night,* Luther focuses on those who are content with their lot, saying,

They stayed in their station and did the work of their
calling. They were pure in heart and content with
their work, not aspiring to be townsmen or nobles, nor
envious of the mighty. Next to faith this is the highest
art — to be content with the calling in which God has
placed you. [...] The best job is the one that you
have. [...] If you are a servant, you are in the very
best position. Be diligent and know that there are no
greater saints on this earth than servants.[41]

In the Wise Men, Luther admires their ability
to look past "all that glitters in the world and look
rather on the despised and foolish things, help the
poor, comfort the despised, and aid the neighbor in
his need."[42] The Magi were able to see Christ where
others saw only poverty, so *they presented him gifts; gold,*
and frankincense and myrrh. In this, Luther finds a
Holy Trinity of hope and faith and love where others
see only material gifts, saying,

> *Thus we see that incense is faith and gold is hope,*
> *because faith believes that all things are and ought to*
> *be of God, and hope accepts and sustains what faith*

*believes. The myrrh is love. Faith takes us from
ourselves, that we should refer everything to God with
praise and gratitude. Hope fills us with the concerns
of others, that we may endure all in patience without
resentment. Love reduces us to that nothing which we
were in the beginning, so that we desire neither goods
nor anything outside of God[....] We can present our
gifts in the same way as the Lord says: "Inasmuch as
ye have done it unto one of the least of these my
brethren, ye have done it unto me."*[43]

And the Christ-child is, of course, Grace
incarnate, the sole-begotten Son of God, born of the
Virgin Mary. *For unto you is born this day in the city of
David a Saviour, which is Christ the Lord.* Luther invites
us, finally, to contemplate the spiritual significance
of the Nativity:

*Mary is the figure of Christianity, that is, all
Christians who wrap the newborn Child in the word
of the Gospel. The swaddling clothes signify the
preaching of the Gospel; the manger signifies the place*

where Christians come together to hear the word of God. The ox and ass stand for us.[44]

Fortunately, the ox and ass can keep time, since, in addition to his homilies, Luther was instrumental in bringing congregational singing into the church. In fact, he is often quoted as echoing Saint Augustine in exclaiming, *One who sings prays twice!* Luther himself composed numerous hymns that are still sung today. Besides "A Mighty Fortress Is Our God," for which he is most famous, Luther also wrote the lyrics for five Christmas hymns.

Nevertheless, Luther's carols would ultimately be eclipsed by other German-language Christmas songs such as "O Tannenbaum" ("O Christmas Tree"), which was set to a traditional folk tune, and "Stille Nacht, heilige Nacht" ("Silent Night! Holy Night!"), which was written by Franz Gruber and Joseph Mohr. The latter carol was first performed on Christmas Eve 1818 in Saint Nicholas parish church of Salzburg, in what is now Austria, and all who heard the song were immediately enchanted by it. The recording of "Silent Night" sung by Bing Crosby in 1935 is the fourth best-selling song of all time, and in 2011, the song was declared an intangible cultural heritage by UNESCO.

Silent night! Holy night!
Son of God, love's pure light
Radiant beams from Thy holy face,
With the dawn of redeeming grace,
Jesus, Lord at Thy birth,
Jesus, Lord at Thy birth.[45]

AND ONCE THE PEOPLE of Germany found their voice, they spilled out of the churches and into the streets, sending the soul of Saint Nicholas aloft once more as they strolled along, caroling in joyous harmony. One of those carolers was a young boy named Johann Sebastian Bach, whose fine soprano was highly valued. Sebastian was born and raised in the town of Eisenach, in the shadow of towering Wartburg Castle, where an exiled Martin Luther had translated the Bible's New Testament into the

Saxony dialect of German nearly two hundred years before. Though tragically orphaned by the age of ten, Sebastian utilized his voice and burgeoning skills on violin and pipe organ to embark on a musical career that would see him performing and composing in courts and churches throughout the land, culminating in his post as *Thomaskantor* in Leipzig, the Saxony hub of education, trade, and commerce, and the site of Luther's reformation proclamation in 1539. The position of Thomas cantor had since become one of the most highly respected positions in Lutheran Protestantism as it required directing and performing sacred music at Leipzig's two most important churches: Saint Thomas and — need we say it? — Saint Nicholas.

Nikolaikirche, or Saint Nicholas Church, had been established in 1165 AD, more than 500 years before Bach's arrival in 1723. It was first built in the medieval Romanesque style, not unlike the Basilica di San Nicola back in Bari, Italy; then it was extended and enlarged in the Gothic style with the rib vaults and stained glass windows common to cathedrals of the 16th century. Among the many notable German figures who attended Saint Nicholas Church was G.W. Leibniz, who was baptized there on the 23rd of June 1646. The christening of baby Gottfried, which means "God-peace," was attended by theologians and professors of the nearby University of Leipzig, and it was reported that at the very moment of his baptism the newborn "raised his head with wide open eyes," a clear sign of his "exceptional future contribution to the glory of God and the advancement of the church."[46] Little Götz would later attend *Nikolaischule,* or Saint Nicholas School, where the young polymath soon surpassed even the teachers in his understanding of Latin and classical logic. From Saint Nicholas, the foremost founder of the Enlightenment went on to explain the binary number system, upon which today's computing technology is based; invent the first working mechanical calculator that performed all four arithmetic functions (i.e., addition, subtraction, multiplication, and division); devise a digital computer that would utilize gravity where we now use electricity; and, as co-inventor with Sir Isaac Newton, develop the notation that we still use in that branch of mathematics known as the calculus. These achievements notwithstanding, Leibniz felt his true calling was in philosophy, to which he contributed the idea of universal, pre-established harmony and his theory of *monads,* which he often likened to the soul. In his greatest philosophical statement, "The Monadology," Leibniz concludes:

> *These principles have given me a way of naturally explaining the union, or rather the conformity of the soul and the organic body. The soul follows its own laws and the body also follows its own; and they agree in virtue of the harmony pre-established between all substances, since they are all representations of a single universe.*[47]

Additionally, Leibniz was preoccupied with "genuinely *pure love,* which takes pleasure in the happiness of the beloved."[48] Only in this way, the

43

Saint Nicholas graduate believed, could universal harmony be observed on earth. In his *Demonstratio Propositionum Primarum,* Leibniz would elucidate by using a logic chain thusly: "*Wisdom* is the science of happiness. [...] A *good man* is one who loves all human beings. *To love* is to find delight in the happiness of another. To find delight is to feel harmony."[49] Saint Nicholas must surely be proud of such a protégé.

While on the subject of harmony, it should also be noted that it was Leibniz who famously said, "Music is the hidden arithmetical exercise of a mind unconscious that it is calculating."[50] Which brings us back to Old Bach. It has been suggested that, because "numeracy was not taught as a separate discipline" in the late 17th century, Bach may have sensed that, since God obviously created numerically, music must, therefore, adhere to "the natural manifestations of mathematical law."[51] Musical structure, or *harmonia,* should ultimately imitate the structure of nature and its Creator; that is,

"Music is a mixed mathematical science that concerns the origins, attributes, and distinctions of sound, out of which a cultivated and lovely melody and harmony are made, so that God is honored and praised but mankind is moved to devotion, virtue, joy, and sorrow."[52] As Georg Venzky, who, like Bach, was a member of Lorenz Christoph Mizler's Society of Musical Science, explains: "God is a harmonic being. All harmony originates from his wise order and organization[....] Where there is no conformity, there is also no order, no beauty, and no perfection. For beauty and perfection consists in the conformity of diversity."[53] In this musical principle of unity in diversity we hear echoes of an Augustinian trinity of Unity, Equality, and Harmony — the very principle that Nicholas of Myra successfully championed at the First Council of Nicaea.

IT SHOULD COME AS no surprise, then, that the greatest musical scientist the world has ever known premiered many of his most important sacred compositions at Saint Nicholas Church in Leipzig. Bach's first large-scale work to premiere at Nikolaikirche was his *Passio secundum Joannem,* or *Saint John Passion* (BWV 245), on Good Friday 1724. With this composition, Bach wanted to demonstrate the role that music could play in directing the congregation's thoughts to the meaning of Christ's Passion in their own lives. As the eminent conductor and musicologist John Eliot Gardiner points out, "the multilayered structure underpinning Bach's Passion can be 'felt,' if not immediately seen or heard, by the listener, in the same way that flying buttresses, invisible to the visitor when entering a Gothic church [such as Nikolaikirche], are essential to the illusion of lightness, weightlessness and the impression of height."[54] Thus Saint Nicholas Church was the perfect venue for Bach to present "his own first triumphant vindication of Luther's injunction that 'Christ's Passion must be met not with words or forms, but with life and truth.'"[55] In

Bach, we encounter Christ's Passion through unity in diversity, the science of harmony.

Over the next several years, the "progenitor of harmony," as Ludwig van Beethoven would later dub J.S. Bach, premiered numerous chorales and Christmas cantatas at Saint Nicholas Church, culminating in his *Christmas Oratorio* (BWV 248), first presented on Christmas Day 1734. As Christoph Wolff notes, "Having harmonized over the decades hundreds of chorales and having taught the skill to scores of students, Bach still found it possible to break through even his own conventions. For the chorale settings of the *Christmas Oratorio* reveal a new degree of polyphonic sophistication, elegance of voice leading, and immediacy of expression."[56] The opening Chorus of Bach's oratorio might well be sung in praise of the composer himself:

Shout for joy, exult, rise up, glorify the day,
praise what today the highest has done!
Abandon hesitation, banish lamentation,
begin to sing with rejoicing and exaltation!

Serve the highest with glorious choirs,
let us honour the name of our ruler!

BACH WOULD GO ON to produce even greater
works, including his *Saint Matthew Passion* (BWV 244)
and the glorious *Mass in B Minor* (BWV 232), the
latter of which also premiered at Saint Nicholas
Church. Later in life, he would return to performing
and composing primarily keyboard works, most
notably *The Art of Fugue,* in which he attained the
pinnacle of contrapuntal composition. After his
death, however, Bach quickly faded from collective
memory, a phenomenon that was helped in no small
part by the success of two of his sons, C.P.E. Bach
and J.C. Bach, whose fame and fortune in Baroque
music far surpassed that of their father. In fact, Old
Bach might have been forgotten entirely if it had not
been for the providential discovery of some of
Bach's manuscripts by a student at the University of
Leipzig named Felix Mendelssohn. It was
Mendelssohn's revival of the *Saint Matthew Passion,*

performed by the Berlin Singakademie in 1829, that finally released the soul of J.S. Bach into the wider world, which has held him in the highest esteem ever since. As for Mendelssohn himself, the early Romantic composer would go on to compose many well-known works, but without doubt his most popular composition is the music to "Hark, the Herald Angels Sing," which he wrote in 1840.

> **Hark! The herald angels sing,**
> **"Glory to the newborn King;**
> **Peace on earth and mercy mild,**
> **God and sinners reconciled!"**[57]

THEN DARKNESS DESCENDED UPON the land. After their humiliating defeat in World War I, a nationalist fervor gripped all of Germany, and the National Socialist Party, or Nazis, rose to power with dreams of German domination based on delusions of ethnic superiority. Following the *Kristallnacht* riots of November 1938, in which Nazis destroyed the property of their Jewish neighbors, concentration camps were established throughout the region: Bergen and Buchenwald, Sachsenhausen and Dachau. Jews were arrested and detained; atrocities were committed, from starvation to slave labor to torture in the name of science to mass murder: genocide. If Felix Mendelssohn, who was descended from Jewish ancestry, had still been alive, he too would likely have been persecuted, imprisoned, and possibly even killed. God and sinners were estranged. Then came World War II, a time of no peace anywhere on earth. Many German churches were destroyed in Allied bombing raids, yet Leipzig's Nikolaikirche survived. In the wake of the war, Saxony became part of East Germany, which was governed by Marxists who suppressed religion — the opiate of the masses — in the name of secular values. The soul of Saint Nicholas was very nearly snuffed out. Yet some embers still smoldered.

Agitated by communist oppression and a faltering economy, Leipzigers began coming together on Monday evenings in the fall of 1989. People met

on the square located between Saint Nicholas
Church and Saint Nicholas School, and their
numbers quickly grew. By October, it had become
known as the Monday Demonstrations, and
thousands of people gathered at Saint Nicholas each
week, holding lit candles aloft and chanting, "No
violence!" and "We are the people!" On Monday,
October 9, 1989, their numbers swelled to an
estimated 70,000 people. They spilled out into the
streets of Leipzig, a river of candlelight flowing
through the dark of night. The Peaceful Revolution
had begun, and it soon spread across all of East
Germany. The Berlin Wall came down, and the Iron
Curtain was *rent in twain from the top to the bottom,*
marking the end of the Cold War between Eastern
Bloc and Western Bloc nations. Soviet communism
would soon collapse as well, and it all began at the
church of Saint Nicholas — the people's victory.

AT THIS POINT, WE might expect the journey
to continue eastward, into Mother Russia, but we

would be surprised to find that the soul of Saint Nicholas had been there all along, having long ago escaped Turkish invasion by flying out of the Great Gate of Constantinople and into the Great Gate of Kiev, then settling comfortably under the colorful onion domes of the Russian Orthodox Church, from the shores of the Baltic Sea in the west through the vast taiga forests of Siberia to the Bering Strait, where each new day begins, far to the east. As the patron saint of Russia, Nicholas is the most beloved of saints and is second only to Saint Mary in veneration. On Thursdays all liturgical prayers are directed to *Nikola* as representative of all the saints. Russians like to say, "If anything happens to God, we've always got Saint Nicholas." Christmas was banned under Communist rule; however, Saint Nicholas Day, celebrated on the Sixth of December, remained an important date on the Russian calendar. Customs vary across Russia, but in many homes, Saint Nicholas brings gifts to the children who've been good. In some regions he brings a rod for parents to discipline the kids who've been bad, and he is often accompanied by both an Angel and a Devil.

If Germany is known for its Christmas carols, then Russia is renowned for its ballet; and the best beloved Russian ballet is undoubtedly *The Nutcracker* by Pyotr Ilyich Tchaikovsky. In this two-act ballet, we enter the German home of a little girl named Clara on Christmas Eve. Her parents are throwing a Christmas party for the children and a few guests, including Clara's godfather, Herr Drosselmeyer, a magician whose assistant has brought an Angel for the top of the Christmas tree. When the tree is lighted, a real Christmas Angel momentarily appears in front of the tree, but only Clara can see it. Following a visit from Saint Nicholas, Herr Drosselmeyer presents the children with gifts. To Clara he gives a wooden nutcracker, which is actually his handsome nephew, transformed into the Nutcracker by an evil spell. While the children are dancing, Clara's brother Fritz, jealous of her gift, grabs the nutcracker and breaks it. Drosselmeyer repairs the toy with a kerchief then leaves, as the clock is about to strike midnight. Clara tucks the Nutcracker into her doll's bed; but when she checks on him again, the Christmas Angel reappears and beckons Clara to follow her downstairs, into the frightening darkness below, where toys suddenly come to life and the Christmas tree grows enormously. Clara dances with the Nutcracker, her hero, until the Christmas Angel again appears and leads them into the Land of Snow, where sparkling snowflakes are dancing. Her godfather reappears and takes the young couple in his horse-drawn sleigh to the next stop in their journey, the Kingdom of Sweets. The Sugar Plum Fairy welcomes them, and they are treated to a montage of tasty delights from across the Eurasian world: tantalizing chocolate from Spain, sensual coffee from Arabia, sprightly tea from China, and vigorous candy canes from Kiev. The Rose Fairy and other blossoms dance the Waltz of the Flowers, and the climax is a *pas de deux* by the

Sugar Plum Fairy and her Prince. Drosselmeyer appears once more to lay the sleeping Clara at the foot of the clock then disappears again. When Clara awakens on Christmas Day, she rushes outside wearing only her nightgown to find her godfather but instead runs into his nephew, now a handsome human version of the Nutcracker, who wraps her in his cloak. In Tchaikovsky's coming-of-age story, Drosselmeyer has secretly given Clara the gift of love as a reward for overcoming her fear of darkness. In return, she gives her godfather the gift of his transformed nephew. When the story is read, the theological symbolism is not hard to spot. That it can be brought to life in the minds of "kids from one to ninety-two" through music and dance alone is truly remarkable.

When *The Nutcracker* premiered in St. Petersburg, in December 1892, it inspired tepid audience reactions, and worse reviews, yet it has gone on, through various adaptations and modifications, to become a holiday favorite around the globe. For many people, *The Nutcracker* is their first and often their only encounter with ballet, while for many ballet companies, the annual production of *Nutcracker* is what enables them to keep dancing through the rest of the year.

FROM ST. PETERSBURG, THE SOUL of Saint Nicholas would leap as in a *grand jeté* to the west, flying with the sun across the Gulf of Finland, along the Arctic Circle, and into Scandinavia, where Laplanders had long told tales of magicians who cross the night sky with flying reindeer, a land where elfen folk are everywhere performing deeds mischievous or helpful, depending upon their mood. Every home in Scandinavia is said to have at least one Christmas elf known as *Julenisse* (in which *Jul* means Yule, for Yuletide or Christmastime, and *Nisse* is an archaic variant of Nicholas). These Christmas elves wear pointy red hats and spend most of the year hiding in dark corners of the home, but at Christmas they come out to play tricks on little children. In order to keep the elves in good humor, Swedish kids have learned over time to place cookies and milk out for them before going to bed on Christmas Eve, thus ensuring that Julenisse will be pleased and leave pleasant gifts in return.[58]

CROSSING THE NORTH SEA for Merrie Olde England, we find that the soul of Saint Nicholas had long been there in the guise of Father Christmas, who may have crossed the English Channel in 1066 AD with the French-Norman troops fighting under William the Conqueror.[59] Boxing Day had been celebrated in England since at least the 17th century, a day when servants of the wealthy were allowed to spend time with their own families and were often presented with a Christmas Box of gifts and food. When gifts were distributed to children, it was traditionally Father Christmas, wearing a red robe and hat, who presented them.

Eventually, the singing of Christmas carols became popular, possibly due to the influence of the

Hanoverian line of monarchs who succeeded to the British throne in 1714.[60] The song known as "Greensleeves" can be traced back to broadsides of the music printed in 1580, and it took on various alternative lyrics from as early as 1686, often ending with the refrain "On Christmas Day in the morning." In 1865, William Chatterton Dix published the version that we know today as "What Child Is This?" in which carolers would wonder aloud at the conditions under which we find the Christ-child:

> **Why lies He in such mean estate,**
> **Where ox and ass are feeding?**
> **Good Christians, fear, for sinners here**
> **The silent Word is pleading.**

AT THE SAME TIME, Queen Victoria carried on the family tradition of her German grandmother, Good Queen Charlotte, who had brought an evergreen tree into the palace for decorating on Christmas Eve since 1800. Soon well-to-do families throughout England wanted to have a fashionable Christmas tree in their own homes as well.

This is the situation that Charles Dickens found himself lamenting in London during the summer of 1843. In spite of appearances, he felt the soul of England was adrift, even as Her Majesty's ships sailed the seven seas, colonizing and Christianizing wherever they landed. Inequities were ubiquitous; despair was everywhere. Coal soot spewed from the smokestacks of Satanic mills and the chimneys of upper-class homes, blanketing London like ashen snow from Hell. Dickens had recently visited Manchester to investigate the working conditions of factories there and was appalled at what he discovered. Even caroling was on the decline, so the soul of Saint Nicholas had diminished to little more than a whisper. Worse, Dickens himself was on the brink of bankruptcy, and his wife was expecting their fifth child.

Then Dickens visited the Field Lane Ragged School, an organization dedicated to providing free

Christian education for the city's most destitute children, children whose ragged appearance, malodorous clothing, and unruly behavior would make them unwelcome in any other church or school situation. Dickens was deeply moved by the deprivation he witnessed among the ragged pupils there. Though his own childhood had been exceedingly difficult — he spent much of it indentured to a shoe-blacking factory while his father languished in the Marshalsea debtor's prison — Dickens realized that he had been far more fortunate than the children he saw at Field Lane Ragged School. So Dickens resolved to do something about it. All of it.

He would write a story, a story so touching that all who read it would be moved to charitable acts, yet so simple that anyone could readily see its point, even a child. He would bring back the spirit of Christmas by incorporating carols into the story. No, more than that, the story itself would be a Christmas carol. That's it! *A Christmas Carol!* Now all he had to do was write it. For six weeks, Dickens was wholly absorbed in writing his novella. He composed most of it in his head while taking long walks, wandering the chartered streets of London, then returning home to write, well, like the dickens. And the spirit that drove Dickens to write drove him to tears as well; friends said he would vacillate between openly weeping and hysterically laughing as the story developed in his mind.

The story would be divided into five parts. In less creative hands these would be chapters or acts, but for Dickens they became five *staves:* those sets of five horizontal lines and four spaces on which musical notes are written. The reader would move through events in the plot as though hearing notes in a song — a Christmas carol — with multiple characters sounding in a progression of musical chords. Some of the chords are dissonant, others harmonious, while many characters are mere passing tones that advance the contrapuntal carol from points of tension toward resolution by moving stepwise into harmony.

In "Stave One," we meet Ebenezer Scrooge, a character whose surname is now synonymous with stinginess and greed, sitting in his cold counting-house on Christmas Eve, busily laying up his earthly treasure, coinage clinking in time with his counting. Before closing for the day, Scrooge declines an invitation to Christmas dinner with his nephew, dismisses two gentlemen soliciting donations for the poor and destitute — sarcastically asking the gentlemen, "Are there no prisons? Are there no workhouses?" — and derides his employee, Bob Cratchit, for eagerly anticipating a day off from work on the holiday. Scrooge walks home alone and is disturbed by the visage of his former partner, Jacob Marley, dead and buried now these seven years, yet here he is on the doorknocker of Scrooge's home. That night, Marley's Ghost appears wearing the chains of a life spent in miserly greed. The Ghost warns Scrooge that his destiny will be the same if he does not change his ways; then Scrooge counters that Marley was always a good businessman:

"Business!" cried the Ghost, wringing its hands again. "Mankind was my business. The common welfare was my business; charity, mercy, forbearance, and benevolence were, all, my business. The dealings of my trade were but a drop of water in the comprehensive ocean of my business!"[61]

Marley's Ghost then informs Scrooge that he will be haunted by Three Spirits, and without these visits Scrooge cannot hope to avoid the path that Marley's Ghost now treads. The Ghost leaves Scrooge by way of the window, through which Scrooge can now see that the air is "filled with phantoms, wandering hither and thither in restless haste and moaning as they went." And with the choir of phantoms fading into silence, we reach the end of the stave with Scrooge fast asleep.

Who isn't, like Scrooge, easily able to discern the chains that weigh down an associate yet cannot detect the chains of our own making, forged link by link, year after year, by every thought, every word, every deed? *Why beholdest thou the mote that is in thy brother's eye, but considerest not the beam that is in thine own eye?* Habits of mind become habits of heart. They may be good or bad, of course, as measured by the effect they have on ourselves and the world around us, positive or negative. For a flat, one-dimensional character such as Jacob Marley, the links forged will indeed be linear chains, but for children of the Most High such as ourselves, the soul is much more complex. A blank slate at birth, the immortal soul is the tablet upon which a record of all decisions is written in four-dimensional space-time. Every decision is a stitch in the tapestry of the soul, and each tapestry tells a moving story. Just as a mind has thoughts, and the heart has feelings, every soul has stories: the stories that are told; the stories that we create. More than that, the soul is a wake, following its creator through space and time, either amplifying or diminishing the wakes of other souls, and even affecting the environment through which it moves. Every decision creates a new world, for better or for worse. This is the lesson that Scrooge must learn through his Hero's Journey.

So IN "STAVE TWO," Scrooge must be visited by the first of the Three Spirits, just as Marley's Ghost had foretold. The Ghost of Christmas Past, with a bright clear jet of light springing from the crown of its head, has come to show Scrooge how his past has led him to this present. The Spirit first shows him a young boy sitting alone in an empty schoolhouse, a boy whose only friends are characters in the books that he reads. Then the Spirit shows Scrooge a later moment, when his sister Fan comes to take him home for Christmas, "Home for good and all. Home for ever and ever. Father is so much kinder than he used to be, that home's like Heaven!" Scrooge is reminded that he lost contact with his lovely sister, who bore one child before she died, Scrooge's nephew.

Next the Spirit transports them to a Christmas party thrown by his former employer, Fezziwig. Scrooge sees his former self as an apprentice having a grand time with friends in the company of old Fezziwig's generous Christmas spirit. When they listen in on the younger Scrooge and another apprentice praising Fezziwig, the Spirit says, "Why! Is it not? He has spent but a few pounds of your mortal money: three or four, perhaps. Is that so much that he deserves this praise?"

"It isn't that," said Scrooge, heated by the remark, and speaking unconsciously like his former, not his latter self. "It isn't that, Spirit. He has the power to render us happy or unhappy; to make our service light or burdensome; a pleasure or a toil. Say that his power lies in words and looks; in things so slight and insignificant that it is impossible to add and count 'em up: what then? The happiness he gives is quite as great as if it cost a fortune."

The Spirit then transports them to a somewhat older Scrooge, a man in his prime. He is sitting in a parlor with a fair young belle who has tears in her eyes. She tells Scrooge that he has changed; a golden idol has displaced her in his heart. She knows Scrooge will never marry a dowerless girl such as herself, so she releases him to the life he has chosen. Scrooge begs the Spirit to stop, but the Spirit insists upon one shadow more. He takes them into another home, in which the belle, now older, is preparing for Christmas with her charming daughter. Their husband and father comes home and reports that he saw Scrooge working, alone, by candlelight on this Christmas Eve, while his partner Jacob Marley lies on his deathbed, alone. Scrooge sees clearly the theme of loneliness in his life, most of it self-inflicted through self-absorption, and again begs the Spirit to remove him from this place. He tries to extinguish the beam of light that shines forth from the Ghost of Christmas Past and sinks once more into sleep.

Even as children of the Most High, we are also children of human parents and the products of our familial homelife. Though our nurturing will always tint our lives, we are not eternally bound to whatever may have been produced there. Scrooge and his sister Fan are both products of the same abusive home, yet Fan has chosen to forgive and move on, where Scrooge has chosen to wallow in isolation, taking refuge in his books. We see this in Dickens' own biography as well, in which the author overcame a troubled childhood by deciding that he was not going to let it dictate the rest of his life. In fact, he turned disadvantage to his advantage. So even if young Scrooge could not go home for Christmas, he surely could have spent the day with schoolmates or fellow worshippers at church. Then later in life, in spite of the example of Fezziwig, he takes refuge in his accounting books, a decision that changes his whole approach to life and leads him away from a future that he undoubtedly would have found pleasing. *Where your treasure is, there will your heart be also.*

THEN IN "STAVE THREE," Scrooge wakes up with a discordant snore and finds himself in the presence of the Second Spirit, the Ghost of Christmas Present. The Spirit commands Scrooge to touch his robe trimmed with fur, and they set off through the city streets, witnessing people everywhere giddy with excitement in preparing for Christmas. Whenever the mood of passing shoppers would darken, the Christmas Spirit "sprinkled incense" on their dinner or "shed a few drops of water on them" from his most uncommon torch so that everyone's mood was instantly lightened, arousing Scrooge's curiosity.

"Is there a peculiar flavor in what you sprinkle from your torch?" asked Scrooge.

"There is. My own."

"Would it apply to any kind of dinner on this day?" asked Scrooge.

"To any kindly given. To a poor one most."

"Why to a poor one most?" asked Scrooge.

"Because it needs it most."

Could those gifts of Christmas Spirit be frankincense and myrrh water? If so, then all that's missing is gold! The Ghost then leads Scrooge through a series of Christmas scenes, starting with the Cratchit family, who are exultant over their meager Christmas fare, especially Tiny Tim, their crippled child, who exclaims "God bless us every one!" and who, with his plaintive little voice, leads the family in singing a song about a lost child travelling in the snow.

Scrooge and the Ghost next fly west to a dismal mining village, where they behold a family of four generations in a tiny hut of mud and stone as the elder of their little clan "in a voice that seldom rose above the howling of the wind upon the barren waste, was singing them a Christmas song; it had been a very old song when he was a boy; and from time to time they all joined in the chorus. So surely as they raised their voices, the old man got quite blithe and loud; and, so surely as they stopped, his vigour sank again." They fly out to a solitary lighthouse where two watchmen warm themselves over a fire, join hands and wish each other a Merry Christmas, then strike up a "sturdy song that was like a gale in itself." They fly further west, out to sea, and witness a ship's crew far from any shore "but every man among them hummed a Christmas tune, or had a Christmas thought, or spoke below his breath to his companion of some bygone Christmas-day, with homeward hopes belonging to it."

Finally, they fly into the home of Scrooge's nephew, who is entertaining guests with his exceedingly pretty wife. There was plenty of musical talent in that little group, and they sang and played "among other tunes, a simple little air (a mere nothing: you might learn to whistle it in two minutes), which had been familiar to the child who fetched Scrooge from the boarding-school, as he had been reminded by the Ghost of Christmas Past." The party plays a game of blindman's buff, in which the "blindman," Topper, did not seem to be entirely blind, and the plump sister-in-law of Scrooge's nephew did not seem displeased at being caught. Then Scrooge's nephew leads everyone in a game of Yes or No, in which they have to guess what he's thinking, and all of their binary answers lead them to the truth: the disagreeable, savage animal that growls and grunts sometimes, and talks sometimes, and lives in London, and walks about the streets, and is neither horse nor ass nor cow, nor bull nor tiger, nor dog nor pig is none other than his Uncle Scrooge, whom they then toast. "A merry Christmas and a happy New Year to the old man, whatever he is!"

Much they saw, and far they went, and many homes they visited, but always with a happy end. The Spirit stood beside sick-beds, and they were cheerful; on foreign lands, and they were close at home; by struggling men, and they were patient in their greater hope; by poverty, and it was rich. In almshouse, hospital, and gaol, in misery's every refuge, where vain man in his little brief authority had not made fast the door, and barred the Spirit out, he left his blessing, and taught Scrooge his precepts.

Then, as chimes are ringing the late hour, by which the Ghost of Christmas Present must depart, Scrooge notices something protruding from the hem of his robe. The Spirit moves the folds to reveal two wretched little children, a boy and a girl: Ignorance and Want.

"Have they no refuge or resource?" cried Scrooge.

"Are there no prisons? said the Spirit, turning on him for the last time with his own words. "Are there no workhouses?"

And the Ghost was gone, but through the mist Scrooge can just make out a "solemn Phantom, draped and hooded," coming toward him, and he knows with dread certainty who it must be.

Before we can meet the future, however, we should look more closely at the present, in which the Ghost of Christmas Present has shown Scrooge a series of harmonious situations where we would not expect to hear harmony. Whether *A Christmas Carol* was inspired by what Dickens wanted to write in "Stave Three" or vice versa, we do not know;

however, these multiple scenes of people singing carols are certainly pivotal in the structure of Dickens' novella. Like Luther and Bach before him, Dickens clearly sees the benefit in choral singing, no matter how woeful the situation. The spherical nature of sound centers us, creating a feeling of oneness. When that experience is shared with others, unity is transformed into equality and, ultimately, harmony.

NOW BACK TO "STAVE FOUR." The Phantom slowly, gravely, silently approaches Scrooge, for that is how the future arrives. There is no sleeping, no pleasant cessation of awareness, as between past and present. The future meets our eternal present right now, where we are. We can see it coming, of course, but it remains shrouded. It will not speak to us. Instead it leads us straight into the circumstances determined by the present. For Scrooge, this is first into a group of fellow businessmen who are airily dismissive of the death of an associate whose upcoming funeral is a burden on their busy lives. Another group of businessmen exchange pleasantries yet make no mention of the death of their associate. Then Scrooge realizes that his associates are all gathered according to their — and his — daily routines, but he is not among them as he always had been.

The Ghost of Christmas Yet to Come then leads Scrooge to a back-alley pawnshop, where an unsavory crew is laughing, seeking to hock some wares to old Joe, the greasy pawnbroker. The undertaker's helper produces his plunder first: "a seal or two, a pencil-case, a pair of sleeve-buttons, and a brooch of no great value." The laundress tosses in "sheets and towels, a little wearing apparel, two old-fashioned silver tea-spoons, a pair of sugar-tongs, and a few boots." Finally, the charwoman presents a bundle of bed-curtains and blankets. "I hope he didn't die of anything catching? Eh?" says old Joe. The pawnbroker pays these would-be tomb raiders for their booty, and Scrooge cries, "Spirit! I see, I see. The case of this unhappy man might be my own. My life tends that way now. Merciful Heaven, what is this?" And they are instantly beside a bed, "a bare, uncurtained bed: on which, beneath a ragged sheet, there lay a something covered up, which, though it was dumb, announced itself in awful language." It is, of course, a corpse.

The Phantom takes Scrooge to the home of a couple who owed Scrooge money. With any luck, their debt may not be transferred, as there was no heir to the estate of Scrooge and Marley, "and it was a happier house for this man's death!" Scrooge begs the Phantom to show him "some tenderness connected to a death," so he conducts them through the streets to Bob Cratchit's home, where the family is mourning the loss of their dear Tiny Tim. The whole family reminisces fondly, and Cratchit tells his wife that even Scrooge's nephew offered his assistance in their time of grief. The Phantom takes Scrooge back out into the street, presumably to go home, but instead leads him to the court of a church and through the iron gate, where the bony finger of Time points at a headstone bearing the inscription EBENEZER[62] SCROOGE. Scrooge repents of his past and senses some relenting on the part of the Ghost of Christmas Yet to Come, as its "kind hand trembled." On his knees, Scrooge prays,

I will honour Christmas in my heart, and try to keep it all the year. I will live in the Past, the Present, and the Future. The Spirits of all Three shall strive within me. I will not shut out the lessons that they teach. Oh, tell me I may sponge away the writing on this stone!

Scrooge takes the hand of the Phantom, but it rebuffs him. "Holding up his hands in a last prayer to have his fate reversed, he saw an alteration in the Phantom's hood and dress. It shrunk, collapsed, and dwindled down into a bedpost." And Scrooge was on his knees beside it.

By following in the wake of the soul of Saint Nicholas we behold a Trinity of Trinities. Viewed horizontally, we saw first the Augustinian trinity of Unity, Equality, and Harmony; next the Lutheran trinity of Hope, Faith, and Love; and now the Dickensian trinity of Past, Present, and Future. Viewed vertically they become Unity through Hope in the Past, Equality through Faith in the Present, and Harmony through Love in the Future: the gifts of the Magi.

WELL, SCROOGE WOULD NOT be much of a hero if he did not get right up off his knees and resurrect himself, a true prodigal son, as *it is easier for a camel to go through the eye of a needle, than for a rich man to enter into the kingdom of God,* yet in "Stave Five" that is exactly what he does. "'I will live in the Past, the Present, and the Future! Scrooge repeated as he scrambled out of bed. 'The Spirits of all Three shall strive within me.'" Noting that his bed still has curtains, Scrooge realizes he can still make amends. He bids a boy in the street to go and purchase the prize turkey that's hanging in the window of the corner butcher shop, and tips him handsomely when the boy promptly does so. He has the turkey delivered anonymously to Bob Cratchit's house for their Christmas dinner, and he pays a cab to take the butcher there. He dresses with a chuckle and fairly skips out into the street, where he runs into one of the two gentlemen who tried and failed to solicit a donation from him the day before, but today Scrooge discreetly pledges a generous gift in behalf of the poor and the destitute. He goes to church and walks the streets like Nicholas of Myra, taking pleasure in all that he sees. Finally, he winds up at his nephew's house for Christmas dinner and makes himself right at home. "Wonderful party, wonderful games, wonderful unanimity, won-der-ful happiness!" The next day, he would give Bob Cratchit a raise in pay, and over the years he would be like a second father to Tiny Tim, who did NOT die, and "it was always said of him that he knew how to keep Christmas well, if any man alive possessed the knowledge. May that be truly said of us, and all of us! And so, as Tiny Tim observed, God bless Us, Every One!"[63]

So ends *A Christmas Carol,* Charles Dickens' most beloved work. Dickens felt strongly that his story must be presented in a manner befitting its stature, so when his publisher refused to provide for more than a plain and inexpensive printing, Dickens used his own diminishing funds to hire an illustrator and have the book properly bound in a handsome cover. The novella was a bestseller from the moment it hit the bookstores on December 19, 1843, quickly selling out all 6,000 copies of its initial print run. Unfortunately, it did not have the effect of lifting Dickens out of his financial straits, as sales did little more than offset his lavish printing expenses. Nevertheless, his story cemented the author in readers' hearts on both sides of the Atlantic, and his situation would soon improve through subsequent works. The story itself then took on a life of its own. It was adapted for the stage shortly after its initial publication, and screen adaptations have been produced since the early days of motion pictures. The BBC has adapted it for radio, and Marcel Marceau even performed it in mime on television.

In this way, *A Christmas Carol* clearly demonstrates the effect that a soul can have on the world. Dickens' decision to portray the spirit of charitable giving has had an inestimable impact on generations of Scrooges — that is, all of us — and who knows how many of the poor and destitute have received assistance as a result. At the same time, the story is itself an echoing ripple effect of the soul of Saint Nicholas. The Ghost of Christmas Present (note the double entendre) is a literary take on Father Christmas, which is English for *Père Noël,* otherwise known as Saint Nicholas, the spirit of secret almsgiving. The Ghost of Christmas Past is simply the integration of all previous iterations of the Ghost of Christmas Present, a spiritual line that stretches back to Patara and, ultimately, to Bethlehem, where the Magi offered gold and frankincense and myrrh: hope and faith and love.

And for a time anyway, Dickens' yearning to reestablish carol singing was fulfilled, though in recent years we seem to prefer delegating such singing to an elite class of professionals. Aside from singing "Happy Birthday" and the national anthem, our society has largely given up choral singing. Nonetheless, the professionals have done well in providing us with an annual dose of carols. English progressive rock musician Greg Lake penned a popular Christmas song for Emerson, Lake, and Palmer with "I Believe in Father Christmas," which reached the number two spot on the UK Singles Chart in 1975 (behind Queen's "Bohemian Rhapsody," which reigned at number one for nine weeks). Lake would later note, "Whether you believe in Christianity or not, Christmas is a time of hope, when many of us try to put our troubles to one side and concentrate a little harder on goodwill."[64] In Lake's song we hear a postmodern echo of the soul of Saint Nicholas, retracing its wake to the Nativity and back again:

They sold me a dream of Christmas

They sold me a Silent Night

They told me a fairy story

Till I believed in the Israelite

And I believed in Father Christmas

And I looked at the sky with excited eyes

'Till I woke with a yawn,

in the first light of dawn

And I saw him through his disguise

JUST WHO IS DISGUISED in Lake's lyric is ambiguous. Whether it's him or Him, or Christ or his father, is irrelevant: all are connoted by "Father Christmas." And with that, the soul of Saint Nicholas flew on across the Irish Sea, landing upon the tempest-tossed shores of the Emerald Isle, where we are again surprised to discover that Nicholas is already there.

Remember how hastily the 47 knights of Bari raided the tomb of Nicholas back in 1087 AD? Well, as it turns out, one of his successors in the bishopric at Myra was completely consumed with covetous envy of his illustrious predecessor. This man was so sick of constantly hearing about "Nicholas this" and "Nicholas that," with everybody continually going on and on about "Nicholas, Nicholas, Nicholas" that while on his deathbed he demanded to be buried in the same sepulcher so that he would forever remain above the object of his envy, that infuriating do-gooder, Nicholas. So when the Italian knights of Bari rushed into the church, intent upon beating the Venetians to their treasure, they hastily scooped up the first bones they could find and unwittingly exhumed the Bishop of Envy, leaving Nicholas alone once more in his sepulcher.

Not long afterward, some Crusaders, knights returning from the Holy Land, felt themselves called to protect their beloved Nicholas from marauding Turks. So in 1200 AD they transferred his sacred relics from Myra to the Church of St. Nicholas in County Kilkenny, in the south of Ireland, where the saint now rests in peace among the many monastic ruins found there.

YET THE SOUL OF Saint Nicholas flew onward still, westward, utilizing great circle navigation to chart a polar route toward the New World, that youthful beacon of hope, the United States of America. It was the Dutch immigrants settling in New Amsterdam (now known as New York) who first brought their Sinterklaas to these shores in the 17th century. As the Dutch were joined by increasing numbers of German and English immigrants, *Sinterklaas* became *Santeclaus,* and finally *Santa Claus,* where *Claus* rhymes not with "house" and the German "Klaus" but with "pause" (or possibly "paws"). Only in America could the feminine form *santa* be used to address a male saint, yet the androgynous appellation does serve to reinforce the ambiguity of Santa. If the United States is a metaphorical melting pot, then Santa Claus is the figure that arises from that American crucible.

Though he seems to have left Black Pete and his mitre behind back in Holland, Santa Claus soon adopted the elves and a pointy red hat from Sweden, so children of Swedish immigrants were inclined to set out some cookies and milk for him. The Russians donated their ballet and a sleigh, while Finns provided a team of reindeer to pull it. The French taught their children to hang stockings on the fireplace mantel in faithful anticipation. The German immigrants still sang their Christmas carols, so the British staged *A Christmas Carol.*

WITH THE PUBLICATION OF "A Visit from St. Nicholas" (a.k.a. "'The Night before Christmas") by Clement Clarke Moore in 1823, Santa's big night was officially moved from Saint Nicholas Day, usually celebrated on the 6th of December, to Christmas Eve. We also learned that Santa's eight reindeer have names: *Dasher, Dancer, Prancer, Vixen, Comet, Cupid, Donner,* and *Blitzen.* Harnessing his team from a variety of English, Latin, and German words connoting speed, power, and grace, Santa's sleigh is thus pulled by the mythical magic of artists, animals, a celestial visitor, thunder, lightning, and, of course, love. The German-born political cartoonist Thomas Nast next outfitted Moore's jolly old elf in a red fur-trimmed jacket, broad black belt and boots, and decided that Santa must spend most of the year in his workshop up at the North Pole, which had recently captivated the American imagination through polar expeditions such as those led by Robert Peary and supported by the increasingly popular National Geographic Society. Nast also depicted Santa with a list of children naughty and nice, and stacks of letters from credulous kids around the world.[65] Finally, in 1931, a Swedish-American pin-up artist named Haddon "Sunny" Sundblom painted the rotund and rosy-cheeked Santa Claus that we know today for a series of Coca-Cola ads in which the merrily mirthful Santa would hold children on his lap, play with electric trains (the high-tech toys of the early 20th century), and raid the refrigerator (the latest in modern household appliances), always while enjoying a bottle of Coke.[66] And with that, a thoroughly American icon was born.

THOUGH IT MAY SEEM that solidifying the iconography of Santa Claus would spell the end for new portraits, exactly the opposite occurs because, by his very nature, Santa Claus displays fractal characteristics. Fractal geometry shows self-similarity whether in computer-generated images or in nature, where we can see it in billowing clouds, tributaries of river systems, and the branching blood vessels of the human body. Every part resembles the whole, and the whole resembles each part. Nature achieves this through endless repetition: iterative processes of meteorological, geological, or biological development. Fractal mathematics achieves it through self-referencing functions such as $f(z)=z^2+c$ (note that the complex variable z is on both sides of the equation), the recursive function that Benoit Mandelbrot used to create his well-known Mandelbrot set, the iconic image of fractal geometry. As you zoom in and zoom out of the Mandelbrot set, the image always looks similar. The same is true of Santa Claus because the self-referencing function that underlies his fractal image is always the soul of Saint Nicholas: the act of giving in secret. Every soul is, in fact, likewise fractal. Integrity builds character in that consistently walking your talk continuously weaves yet another stitch in the tapestry of your life until there appears a clear image that withstands scrutiny, whether close or far away.

We can see this in Christmas songs that focus on depictions of Santa Claus. Many pick up on clues left by Clement Clarke Moore or Thomas Nast, while others refer to clues from the Bible itself to run the gamut from the juvenile to the burlesque. At one end of the spectrum, we have "Santa Claus Is Coming To Town," a modern nursery rhyme that, like many in this genre, provides an ominous warning for children to heed: "You better watch out / You better not cry / You better not pout." Why? Because crying is inharmonious. Santa Claus is coming and, as the purveyor of good behavior, he expects children to stop exhibiting self-centeredness. An infant may be the center of the universe, but as children grow they must learn to understand the feelings and needs of others around them. Furthermore, as Thomas Nast depicted, Santa keeps a list of who's been "naughty and nice." *He shall come to judge the quick and the dead.* He can do this because he is omniscient: "He sees you when you're sleeping / He knows when you're awake / He knows if you've been bad or good." If you behave and go to sleep, Santa will reward you with gifts so you can wake up in kid heaven. Nevertheless, children should be "good for goodness' sake," which can be taken in several ways. First, it's the kind of idiomatic expression that your grandmother used for emphasis: *Oh, for goodness' sake!* Second, good behavior requires no justification; it's simply the right thing to do. Finally, goodness is fractal, a collective soul that arises iteratively through recursive acts of good behavior, culminating in the kingdom of heaven. *The kingdom of heaven is like unto leaven, which a woman took, and hid in three measures of meal, till the whole was leavened.* Whoever has ears to hear, let them hear.

At the other end of the spectrum, we also enjoy songs that depict a more mischievous Santa Claus. As more American babies are born at the end of summer, it seems the holiday season is not only the most wonderful time of the year, but also the most fertile. Nowhere is this seen more clearly than in the randy anti-Santa portrayed in Brian Setzer's bluesy striptease arrangement of "Santa Claus Is Back In Town":

Hang up your fishnet stockings
Turn off the light baby
Santa Claus is comin'
Down your chimney tonight

NOT ALL AMERICAN CHRISTMAS songs take Santa Claus as their subject, however. Some of the most touching songs reach all the way back to the Nativity for inspiration. In 1941, composer Katherine Kennicott Davis published "Carol of the Drum" as a chorale for amateur choirs. The Trapp Family Singers (of *Sound of Music* fame), recorded the song in 1951; then the Harry Simeone Chorale scored a huge radio hit in 1958 after retitling it "The Little Drummer Boy." Davis had set her ballad to a traditional Czech melody, so to contemporary ears the tune sounds ancient, as though it could have been written in the year 1 AD. What really makes it work, though, is the text. Using simple language interspersed with echoic "pa-rum-pum-pum-pum" to imitate a drum, the speaker of the poem recounts his own Hero's Journey, which takes place beside the manger where Infant Jesus lay.

The little drummer begins with a clear Call to Adventure, "Come, they told me," in which the Magi invite the boy to accompany them as they visit "a newborn King." There is no Refusal of the Call in this Hero's Journey, just the *pa-rum-pum-pum-pum* of his drum before, Crossing the Threshold, the boy enters his Special World, a stable wherein he becomes a previously unknown character in the Nativity Scene. Having seen the gifts offered by the Magi — gold and frankincense and myrrh — the boy believes he is unworthy. "I am a poor boy too," he says; "I have no gift to bring that's fit to give our King." He screws up his courage anyway and Approaches the Ordeal, humbly asking the Holy Child, "Shall I play for you on my drum?" Receiving no reply to his supplication, the boy looks around for Allies and finds one in Mary, Mother of God. She nods her approval, so he begins to play: *pa-rum-pum-pum-pum*. He wins more Allies as "the ox and lamb kept time": *pa-rum-pum-pum-pum*. "I played my drum for him," he tells us. "I played my best for him." *Pa-rum-pum-pum-pum, rum-pum-pum-pum, rum-pum-pum-pum*. We hear the drums of war as the boy battles with insecurity. We hear his heart pounding as he valiantly confronts his brittle ego. There were no music critics in the house that night, so we have no idea how well the boy actually played during his Ordeal. We don't know if the Magi were tapping their toes in time with the ox and lamb, or smirking behind their *cheches*. But that's not what matters anyway. What matters is that the boy did what he could do. He did it for God. And he did it to the best of his ability. "Then He smiled at me," the boy says, receiving his Reward in apotheosis. If you've ever wondered what it means when the Benediction says, *May the Lord make his face shine upon thee, and be gracious unto thee. May the Lord lift up his countenance upon thee, and give thee peace.* This is it.

The little drummer does not tell us about leaving the stable that night and starting down The Road Back, but we see in his Resurrection that he has gained confidence through a job well done, a gift well received. He Returns with a Boon for the Ordinary World: a story to tell. Like the sailors who told of how Saint Nicholas saw them through their terrors at sea, or better yet, like the tempest-tossed slave trader who finds redemption in "Amazing Grace," every soul has stories, yet the soul of the Little Drummer Boy may hold one of the greatest stories ever told.

And it turns out that the Magi had given the little drummer a gift as well. In addition to the gold and frankincense and myrrh, the hope and faith and love that they offered to Baby Jesus, they may have given the Little Drummer Boy the greatest gift of all: an opportunity. Still, it was up to the little drummer to overcome his reticence, rise to the occasion, and capitalize on the opportunity offered to him. Katherine Davis would go on to leave a similar gift, as she stipulated in her 1980 will that all royalties from "The Little Drummer Boy" would go to the Wellesley College Music Department to support the instruction of instrumental music there. Charity is the gift that keeps on giving.

ONE OF THE MOST visible aspects of charitable giving at Christmastime is the annual Red Kettle campaign of the Salvation Army. On street corners, in shopping malls, and, increasingly, in front of Walmart stores, smiling volunteers ring a bell while attending a red kettle in which passersby can anonymously drop donations for the poor and destitute. Bell Ringers are not required to wear a Santa outfit, yet many do, so the chances of personally sighting the soul of Saint Nicholas on the streets of your town are pretty good. Most donations are small, as people usually drop their change or small bills into the kettle. There are reports, however, of very large donations each year, including anonymous gifts of gold coins, minted symbols of hope, worth thousands of dollars. Red Kettle donations have been solicited by the Salvation Army since 1891, and in recent years they have been used to feed and clothe as many as four-and-a-half million Americans during the holiday season.

WITH THE ADVENT OF television, the soul of Saint Nicholas could fly on invisible beams straight into the American home; no chimney required. It should come as no surprise that the first animated Christmas special produced for TV would be an adaptation of Charles Dickens' holiday favorite. Starring that myopic mumbler who began his career on the silver screen, *Mister Magoo's Christmas Carol* is a musical adaptation of Dickens' novella in which Quincy Magoo is starring in a hit Broadway production of the play. Rather than utilizing Dickens' *stave* structure, the production is a typical three-act play framed by Magoo's chaotic theatre entrance and a curtain call. Otherwise, the 53-minute cartoon stays largely faithful to Dickens, with the exception of the final scene, in which Magoo's Ebenezer Scrooge spends Christmas Day with the Cratchit family rather than with his nephew.

Because it's a musical, we can hear Scrooge's character arc played out in songs that are introduced in Act 1 then reprised in Act 3. In "Ringle, Ringle,"

Magoo's character first sings "Ringle, ringle, coins when they mingle, make such a lovely sound ... Crowns and coppers, little eye poppers, <u>make my pulses pound!</u>" as he lays up his earthly treasure in the counting-house. Then after visits by the Spirits of Christmas, Scrooge literally changes his tune, singing "Ringle, ringle, coins when they jingle, make such a lovely sound ... Crowns and coppers, little eye poppers, <u>were made to pass around!</u>" as he gifts the Cratchits with gold coins from his bag. With Scrooge's newfound generosity, the family is able to purchase and decorate a beautiful Christmas tree while Scrooge sings, "And on this tree, a star of shiny Christmas gold." Then the cast gathers center stage for one last carol, "The Lord's Bright Blessing," and the curtain falls to thunderous applause.

IF MAGOO'S ANIMATED SPECIAL was a first for television, then *A Charlie Brown Christmas* is surely the best beloved. Charles M. Schulz took his

Peanuts characters from the monochrome funny papers to living crayon color on the TV screen in order to let Charlie Brown, his lovable loser, discover what Christmas is all about. And producer Lee Mendelson had the good taste to bring Vince Guaraldi on board to score the cartoon with what would be many kids' first impression of jazz, led by Schroeder at the toy piano. Where Magoo brings Tin Pan Alley to Dickens, the Vince Guaraldi Trio puts the cool in Christmas. And Guaraldi's jazz arrangement of "Greensleeves" is quite possibly the most beautiful ever recorded.

Anyway, Charlie Brown visits his psychiatrist, Lucy, who empathizes with his depression because she never gets what she really wants for Christmas either: real estate. His dog Snoopy is decorating his doghouse for a crass Christmas lights and display contest. His little sister Sally, who cannot yet write, dictates a chatty letter to Santa Claus and ends by suggesting he could make it easy on himself by just sending money: "How about tens and twenties?"

Charlie Brown is exasperated and goes off to join the other kids in putting on a Christmas play as their director. The kids just want to dance to Schroeder playing "Linus and Lucy," the coolest Christmas song ever, and won't take Charlie Brown's direction, so he and Linus go off to buy a Christmas tree for the stage, while Linus frets over memorizing his lines in the play. True to character, Charlie Brown's heart goes out to a loserly little tree that nobody else would buy. In spite of doubts on the part of Linus, Charlie Brown takes the little tree back to the theatre and is met with ridicule and scorn by the other kids. He turns to Linus and asks, "Isn't there anyone who knows what Christmas is all about?" Linus stops sucking his thumb and says, "Sure, Charlie Brown, I can tell you what Christmas is all about." He takes the spotlight and recites:

And there were in the same country shepherds abiding in the field, keeping watch over their flock by night. And, lo, the angel of the Lord came upon them,

and the glory of the Lord shone round about them: and they were sore afraid.

And the angel said unto them, Fear not: for, behold, I bring you good tidings of great joy, which shall be to all people. For unto you is born this day in the city of David a Saviour, which is Christ the Lord. And this shall be a sign unto you; Ye shall find the babe wrapped in swaddling clothes, lying in a manger.

And suddenly there was with the angel a multitude of the heavenly host praising God, and saying, *Glory to God in the highest, and on earth peace, good will toward men.*

Linus exits stage left and says, "That's what Christmas is all about, Charlie Brown"; then he sticks his thumb back in his mouth, having delivered his lines like a pro. Charlie Brown takes his little tree home, where all the other kids help him decorate it with lights and bulbs from Snoopy's prize-winning entry in the Christmas display contest. They gather around the now-glorious Christmas tree, symbol of *harmonia,* the beauty of charitable cooperation, and end by raising their voices in Felix Mendelssohn's "Hark, the Herald Angels Sing."

WE HAVE SO FAR seen two instances of children writing letters to Santa Claus; first in cartoons by Thomas Nast, and now in Sally Brown, who cannot write yet understands the importance of written communication with Santa. This seems rather strange because, unlike Augustine of Hippo, his fellow bishop in the early church, Nicholas of Myra left behind no writing whatsoever. Saint Augustine published voluminous writings, laying the foundations of Christian doctrine and setting standards for Latin rhetoric, the art of persuasive speech. But, for all we know, Nicholas may have been illiterate. Evolving through the centuries, however, due largely, no doubt, to the Lutheran insistence on universal education for all children so

they could learn to read for themselves the Holy
Bible that Martin Luther had translated, the soul of
Saint Nicholas learned to read and write and is now
a prolific author, engaging in correspondence with
children all over the globe.

So in *A Christmas Story* we get a film that takes
this phenomenon to its logical extreme. Ralphie
Parker is a boy who desperately wants something he
knows he can't have for Christmas: a Red Ryder BB
gun. He has already failed in a first attempt at
persuasive speech, when he accidentally blurted out
his desire without properly backgrounding it at the
family dinner table, and his mother immediately shot
it down.

Then his schoolteacher provides Ralphie with
a golden opportunity. She assigns the class a theme
on the topic "What I Want for Christmas."
Unfortunately, Ralphie and Miss Shields soon clash
over issues of form and content. She expects to read
a riveting *exordium* introducing his topic, followed
shortly thereafter by a clear and guiding thesis

statement. She is looking for three or more supporting paragraphs of *confirmatio* and *confutatio,* then a concluding *peroratio* that summarizes his points and ends with a rousing call to action. Instead, Ralphie submits an unstructured stream of desire. He fantasizes that she will fall in love with the author, awarding his work an A++++ and excusing him from theme writing for the rest of the school year. Instead, she gives it a C+, barely above average. Worse, she writes in the margin the most bulletproof counterargument that any kid who wants a BB gun can possibly get: "You'll shoot your eye out!"

Somewhat dubious yet undaunted, Ralphie next tries his luck with a department store Santa Claus, intending to cover his bases, but he gets tongue-tied sitting on the man's knee and can't remember the point of his request, so the grumpy Santa kicks him off the platform.

Christmas morning finally arrives and, despite the cornucopia of gifts under the Christmas tree,

Ralphie is disappointed that he didn't get what he wanted. Then, after the spree of gift opening fervor subsides, his dad notices one more present hidden behind the desk. It's a Red Ryder BB gun. It's not from Santa. It's from his father, who, despite all appearances, had been listening all along. When it comes to supplication, form is not what matters. What matters is who you ask.

EVEN MORE IMPORTANTLY, YOU must believe. *All things are possible to him that believeth.* This is the theme explored in *The Polar Express,* a contemporary classic that rides along with a group of Heroes on a magic train trip to the North Pole. The germ of Chris Van Allsburg's illustrated children's book, published in 1985, is that it simply cannot be true that Santa Claus makes toys for every good boy and girl in a little chalet with a dozen elves as helpers, as had been previously depicted. Santa must actually have a huge manufacturing facility and thousands of elves. He would have to employ the latest technologies. The North Pole, in fact, must be an industrial city like the redbrick textile centers of New England or the automobile producing centers of Michigan, where the story is set, in the middle of the American century. Thus the current technologies include steam locomotives, phonograph recordings, and lighter-than-air craft. The Polar Express carries children who need to learn something about Christmas, about confidence in their belief, to the North Pole so they can discover it in themselves.

In the 2004 film adaptation, Tom Hanks plays six of the archetypes required by a Hero's Journey through motion-capture technology that allows digital animation to be applied to live-action movement of the actor. The protagonist, Hero Boy, is in his "crucial year" [note that *crucial* is derived from the Latin for *cross*]; he wants to believe, but he is harboring doubts — a doubting Thomas. The Conductor is a Mentor responsible for keeping the train on track to meet its rendezvous with Santa Claus at midnight. The Hobo is an Ally who plays devil's advocate, yet he is also puppeteer of the Villain, an Ebenezer Scrooge marionette that incites doubt in Hero Boy's mind. The Father is a Trickster, a magician who wants his children to enjoy the magic of Christmas as long as they can. And Santa Claus is, of course, the soul of Saint Nicholas.

Hero Boy fervently wants to hear sleigh bells indicating Santa's arrival on Christmas Eve, but he is no longer able to hear the bells that other children hear. Just before Santa's departure from the North Pole in his sleigh, one of the bells falls off his reindeer and lands at Hero Boy's feet. Hero Boy picks up the bell and shakes it close to his ear. At first, the bell only echoes Scrooge's words: *"Doubter. Doubter."* Then Hero Boy closes his eyes and says, "I believe. I believe." And the bell rings beautifully and true. Santa Claus appears reflected in the bell and asks, "What was that you said?" Hero Boy says, "I believe. I believe. I believe that this is yours," as he hands the bell to Santa Claus. When Santa Claus later grants the first gift of Christmas to Hero Boy, the boy asks for the sleigh bell, and Santa Claus gives it to him, explaining, "This bell is a wonderful symbol of the spirit of Christmas ... as am I. Just remember, the true spirit of Christmas lies in your heart." But the bell falls out of Hero Boy's torn robe pocket, so he thinks it is lost forever. When he finally returns home, he finds that Santa Claus has not been to his house: there are no presents under the tree; the milk and cookies have not been touched. But the next morning his little sister wakes him, saying, "Wake up. Santa's been here." He follows her downstairs and finds a cornucopia of gifts under the tree, including an electric train set modeled after the Polar Express. Then his sister finds one last present, and it's got his name on it. It's the sleigh bell, accompanied by a note from Santa Claus that reads, "Found this on the seat of my sleigh. Better fix that hole in your pocket. Mr. C." And though the bell eventually falls silent for his friends and little sister, Hero Boy is forever able to hear it ring, *as it does for all who truly believe.*

The film ends with an enchanting image of the sleigh bell reflecting the interior of Hero Boy's home. He has left it on the coffee table in the family's living room, in front of the Christmas plate that previously held cookies, but now holds only a few crumbs. The milk glass is empty too. There is no evidence of Santa's visitation more convincing than a few cookie crumbs and an empty glass of milk. Still, we should reflect upon the significance of the sleigh bell as proof of Hero Boy's adventure.

Unlike Zuzu's petals, which ground George Bailey's physical reality in *It's a Wonderful Life,* the sleigh bell grounds us in the reality of another dimension. In that way, the sleigh bell is more like the two strange white flowers that the Time Traveller brings back from his travels in *The Time Machine* by H.G. Wells. Zuzu's petals are an artifact from the past, hidden to preserve George Bailey's daughter Zuzu's innocence just prior to his crossing the threshold into a special world, where George finds clarity with the help of an angel named

Clarence, who shows George the world as it would be if George — cinema's most heroic anti-Scrooge — had never been born, as if the world had never been touched by the soul of George Bailey.

The Time Traveller's flowers, on the other hand, are an artifact from the future, in which human beings have devolved into two classes, prey and predator, "to witness that even when mind and strength had gone, gratitude and a mutual tenderness still lived on in the heart of man."[67] Similarly, the sleigh bell is an artifact from eternity, an article of faith symbolizing a firmly held belief, a belief in the spirit of Christmas: Christmas Past, Christmas Present, and Christmas Yet to Come.

HOW MANY PARENTS HAVE taken a moment to reflect upon the spirit of Christmas, relaxing and communing, while eating Santa's cookies and drinking his milk (or maybe a glass of wine, having poured the milk back into its carton)? *Do this in remembrance of me.* The stockings are filled with delights from around the world. The Christmas tree twinkles with lights like stars, an evergreen symbol of goodwill and love. The tree is topped with a Christmas Angel or maybe a star of shiny Christmas gold. Beneath its steadfast branches, a foretaste of heaven has been prepared with gifts to spark the imagination and fuel dreams of adventure: crayons and books, a lighted globe of the world or a doll that walks and talks and closes its eyes when it goes to sleep, Lincoln Logs or a bicycle, a Spirograph or an Easy-bake oven, a sleeping bag or musical instrument, a model rocket or maybe even a Polar Express train set. By definition, Santa Claus is always up to date on toy technologies, whether contemporary or traditional, leading edge or retro, and is cognizant of what every child desires and deserves.

Of course, Christmas can be a stressful time as well. The hassle of shopping, wrapping, cleaning, and cooking can take its toll on young parents. The expense of it all is overwhelming. "But we can work harder," says Mr. Claus, "and make next year's Christmas even better." The kids' wants seem insatiable, the in-laws disagreeable. And yet, gazing upon the nativity set, we see that this is how it's always been. Joseph and Mary were as poor as any young couple, yet they made the best of it and bore a child of promise. The children are sleeping, no sound do they make. "Maybe we could have one more," says Mrs. Claus, with a twinkle in her eye. The Magi have left their gifts of hope and faith and love. The shepherds are back at work; the drummer's off playing a gig. The radio reports softly in the background that NORAD's Santa Tracker is heralding the imminent arrival of St. Nicholas. It's time for Mr. and Mrs. Claus to go to bed.

THE NORTH AMERICAN AEROSPACE Defense Command (NORAD) was established by the United States and Canada in the 1950s to provide aerospace warning and protection in the skies over our nations. The Cold War between the Soviet Union and its satellite states and the United States and its allies was deepening, and the threat of long-range bombers and missiles carrying nuclear warheads was keenly felt by all. Air raid shelters were established. Schoolchildren practiced duck-and-cover drills in their classrooms. Tensions ran high. Then in December 1955, something extraordinary happened. The local newspaper in Colorado Springs, Colorado ran a Sears ad with a telephone number that children could call to talk to Santa Claus. There was just one problem: the phone number was for the hotline at NORAD, not the North Pole. When Col. Harry Shoup, commander of NORAD's Combat Alert Center, began receiving calls for Santa Claus, he played along and even assigned some of his airmen to play Santa whenever the hotline rang. Then on Christmas Eve, the airmen drew an image of Santa's sleigh flying south from the North Pole on the blackboard. When Shoup saw the drawing, he immediately phoned a local radio station and reported Santa's departure, which was broadcast throughout the land. The message underlying Shoup's report is clear: our airspace defense systems are so advanced that we can even track Santa Claus; there is no way any enemy bombers or missiles can penetrate our skies. Our children are safe tonight. They can sleep in heavenly peace.

Since that time, the NORAD Santa Tracker has monitored Santa's sleigh in December each year. Utilizing all media, including radio, television, and now the internet, millions of listeners, viewers, and visitors are kept apprised of Santa's real-time movements on the globe as he delivers each Christmas Present. Santa's position is shown on 3D maps accurately depicting planet Earth. He is estimated to fly at 187,500 miles per hour, but therein lies a problem. In Newtonian physics, exact position and velocity cannot be determined simultaneously.

Therefore, it may be more appropriate to utilize quantum mechanics in discussing Santa's flight. Heisenberg's *Uncertainty Principle* tells us that there is a degree of fuzziness in nature; that is, there is a fundamental limit to how precisely we can understand the behavior of certain particles in spacetime. Like an electron orbiting the nucleus of an atom, Santa possesses neither an exact position nor momentum, but instead exhibits a wave function from which the probability of finding him at any given location on Earth can be calculated. Furthermore, we must consider the *observer effect* in determining his whereabouts. If Christ is eternal, then the soul of Saint Nicholas is timely, appearing wherever a need is secretly met. It's like *Schrodinger's cat,* the famous thought experiment originated by Albert Einstein, in which a hypothetical cat may be simultaneously both dead and alive. That is how Santa Claus can both exist and not exist in our homes, our hearts and minds. For, as F. Scott Fitzgerald famously noted, "The test of a first-rate intelligence is the ability to hold two opposed ideas in mind at the same time and still retain the ability to function." Thus, as Einstein taught us, "Imagination is more important than knowledge. For knowledge is limited to all we now know and understand, while imagination embraces the entire world, and all there ever will be to know and understand. Logic will get you from A to B. Imagination will take you everywhere." Which is precisely how Santa Claus flies each Christmas. This principle is applied on the ground, so to speak, by the *imagineers* at Disney Imagineering, who work to realize the wisdom of their founder, Walt Disney: "All our dreams can come true, if we have the courage to pursue them."

THIS WAS MADE ABUNDANTLY clear for us on Christmas Eve 1968. Just four days before Christmas that year, the crew of Apollo 8 blasted off from launchpad 39A at Kennedy Space Center in Florida, becoming the first humans to leave the earth and fly into deep space. They could do this because, only seven years prior, President John F. Kennedy, author of *Profiles in Courage,* had persuasively expressed his belief to the nation in a joint session of

Congress, saying, "I believe that this nation should commit itself to achieving the goal, before this decade is out, of landing a man on the moon and returning him safely to the earth."

In our bid to beat the Soviets to the moon, the mission of Apollo 8 was hastily changed from an Earth orbital type to a flight to the moon. As Apollo 8 Command Module Pilot Jim Lovell later recounted, "It was a bold move. It had some risky aspects to it, but it was a time when we made bold moves."[68] In preparing for Apollo 8's flight, the astronaut sketched a design for the mission patch that would be affixed to their spacesuits: an elongated figure-8 depicting their circumlunar flight path around the earth and the moon on a three-sided patch signifying the conical shape of the Apollo spacecraft. Like a Möbius strip encompassing both Gaia and Luna, the designator "8" is symbolic of their Apollo mission, named for the Sun-god — revealer of past, present, and future, god of sun and light, music and poetry, truth and prophecy. *As above, so below.*

Now it was Christmas Eve, and astronauts Frank Borman, Jim Lovell, and Bill Anders were getting the first look at Earth from the perspective of another heavenly body, the first people to see the entire sphere, the jewel of Earth suspended in the vast and inky blackness of space. "We took photographs as much as we could," Lovell recalled, "and, of course, we took the photograph of the famous Earth rise around the Moon. […] And of course, Christmas Eve, being around the Moon on Christmas Eve, we thought this would be a very auspicious time to say something. The three of us selected to read from the Old Testament, and we had it in fireproof paper in the back of our flight manual."[69] In a radio transmission that was beamed across the universe, the crew recited:

In the beginning God created the heaven and the earth. And the earth

118

was without form, and void; and darkness was upon the face of the deep. And the Spirit of God moved upon the face of the waters. And God said, Let there be light: and there was light.

We close with good night, good luck; a Merry Christmas and God bless all of you, all of you on the good Earth.[70]

WHICH, LIKE SOME LITERARY Möbius strip looping through time and space, brings our story back to where we began: Christmas Eve in Anchorage, Alaska, cold and dark in the bleak midwinter. The stars are brightly shining, yet somber air traffic controllers sit here in darkness, hunched over their radar screens as they sweep the northern skies, staring intently at a phosphorescent blip that's just appeared, blinking like a star on the far horizon. A telephone rings, silver bells pealing through the tense and anxious air.

NORAD's on the line.

Sightings have been confirmed.

The soul of Saint Nicholas is on the way.

THE END

IS NOT YET.[71]

NOTES

---

[1] Doug Joyce, "Anchorage Confirms Santa's Departure," *The Banner-Gazette,* 24 December 1980, front page (archive courtesy of M. Lewis, Campbellsburg, Indiana).

[2] Jacobus de Voragine, *The Golden Legend* (public domain, ms. ca. 1260 AD).

[3] Michael the Archimandrite, *Life of St. Nicholas* (public domain, ms. 9th century AD).

[4] William J. Bennett, *The True Saint Nicholas: why he matters to Christmas* (Brentwood, TN, Howard Books, 2018), 7.

[5] 8.

[6] Jacobus.

[7] Michael.

[8] ibid.

[9] ibid.

[10] ibid.

[11] ibid.

[12] ibid.

[13] Jacobus.

[14] German author unknown, c. 1500, "Es ist ein' Ros' entsprungen," tr. Harriet R. Spaeth, 1875, *The Lutheran Hymnal 645* (St. Louis, MO, Concordia Publishing House, 1941).

[15] Samuel Wesley, Sr., c. 1709, "Behold the Savior of Mankind," *The Lutheran Hymnal 176* (St. Louis,

MO, Concordia Publishing House, 1941).

[16] Bennett, 21.

[17] Michael.

[18] ibid.

[19] Jacobus.

[20] Michael.

[21] ibid.

[22] ibid.

[23] Jacobus.

[24] Michael.

[25] Bennett, 27.

[26] Michael.

[27] "The Nicene Creed," *The Lutheran Hymnal* (St. Louis, MO, Concordia Publishing House, 1941) 22.

[28] Michael.

[29] Jacobus.

[30] ibid.

[31] Bennett, 42.

[32] Jacobus.

[33] Bennett, 89.

[34] 101.

[35] 88-89.

[36] Meister Eckhart, *Selected Writings,* trans. Oliver Davies (New York, Penguin Books, 1994) 116.

[37] 171.

[38] Martin Luther, *Martin Luther's Christmas Book,* ed. Roland Bainton (Minneapolis, MN, Augsburg, 1997) 15.

[39] ibid.

[40] 31.

[41] 35-36.

[42] 59.

[43] 60.

[44] 44.

[45] Franz Gruber and Joseph Mohr, 1818, "Silent Night! Holy Night!" tr. unknown, *The Lutheran Hymnal 646* (St. Louis, MO, Concordia Publishing House, 1941) 3rd verse.

[46] Maria Rosa Antognazza, *Leibniz: An Intellectual Biography,* (New York, Cambridge University Press, 2009), 27.

[47] G.W. Leibniz, *Discourse on Metaphysics and Other Essays,* trans. Daniel Garber and Roger Ariew (Indianapolis, Hackett, 1991) 79.

[48] 81.

[49] Antognazza, 115.

[50] John Eliot Gardiner, *Bach: Music in the Castle of Heaven* (New York, Vintage Books, 2013), 49.

[51] ibid.

[52] John Butt, *Music Education and the Art of Performance in the German Baroque* (Cambridge UP, 1994), 37.

[53] Christoph Wolff, *Johann Sebastian Bach: the Learned Musician* (New York, Norton, 2013), 466.

[54] Gardiner, 394.

[55] 396.

[56] Wolff, 387.

[57] Felix Mendelssohn, 1840, and Charles Wesley, 1739, "Hark! The Herald Angels Sing," *The Lutheran Hymnal 94* (St. Louis, MO, Concordia

Publishing House, 1941) 4th verse.

[58] Bennett, 90.

[59] Recall that Saint Nicholas is known as *Père Noël*, which is French for Father Christmas, in much of France.

[60] The indirect result of G.W. Leibniz having traced the lineage of the German House of Hanover back to the Italian House of Este, by which Duke Georg Ludwig, or George Louis, great-grandson of King James I, sponsor of the first translation of the Bible into English, was allowed to ascend the throne as George I, King of England, Scotland, and Ireland.

[61] Charles Dickens, *A Christmas Carol* (New York, The Baker & Taylor Company, 1905).

[62] Ebenezer comes from the Hebrew *ebhen hā-'ezer*, meaning "stone of help," a commemoration of divine assistance.

[63] ibid.

[64] Greg Lake, *Lucky Man: the autobiography* (London, Constable, 2017), 178.

[65] Bennett, 103.

[66] 104.

[67] H.G. Wells, *The Time Machine* (New York, Dover Publications, Inc., 1995), 76.

[68] David Sington, *In the Shadow of the Moon* (Discovery Films, 2007).

[69] ibid.

[70] ibid.

[71] Matthew 24:6

Made in the USA
Las Vegas, NV
24 November 2020